W9-AHP-224

Picasso

THE LIFE AND WORKS OF

PICASSO

Nathaniel Harris

A Compilation of Works from the
BRIDGEMAN ART LIBRARY

Shooting Star Press Inc
230 Fifth Avenue, New York, New York 10001

Picasso

© Parragon Book Service Ltd 1994

This edition printed for:
Shooting Star Press, Inc.
230 Fifth Avenue - Suite 1212
New York, NY 10001

ISBN   1 56924 177 5

Printed in Italy

Editor: Alexa Stace
Designer: Robert Mathias

The publishers would like to thank Joanna Hartley
at the Bridgeman Art Library for her invaluable help

PABLO PICASSO 1881-1973

PABLO PICASSO, the most famous and also the most versatile artist of the 20th century, was born at Málaga in the south of Spain on 25 October 1881. His father was a drawing master, so Picasso's obvious talent received early recognition, and at fifteen he already had a studio of his own.

After a false start as an art student in Madrid and a bohemian period in Barcelona, Picasso made his first visit to Paris in October 1900. The city was still the artistic capital of Europe, and it became Picasso's permanent home from April 1904, when he moved into the building nicknamed the Bateau-Lavoir (Laundry Boat) in Montmartre, henceforth the new centre of avant-garde art and literature.

During these years Picasso's work was relatively conventional, moving through a mournful Blue Period (1901-05) to the mellower Rose Period (1905). The change of mood may have been prompted in part by his liaison with Fernande Olivier, his first great love. In Picasso's life, women and art were inextricably mixed up together, the appearance of a new woman often signalling a change of artistic direction.

Although his work was becoming commercially successful, Picasso resolutely abandoned his 'Rose' manner. In 1907, inspired by Iberian and African sculpture, he painted *Les Demoiselles d'Avignon* (page 20), one of the great liberating works of modern art. Revelling in a new pictorial freedom, Picasso went on to become co-founder (with the French painter Georges Braque) of Cubism, in which the visible world was deconstructed into its geometrical components. This was arguably the decisive moment at which a fundamental tenet of modern art was established – that the artist's work is not a copy or illustration of the real world, but an addition to it, new and autonomous. Thanks to Cubism, the artist's freedom also extended to materials, so that traditional media such as painting and sculpture could be supplemented or replaced by cut-paper designs, objects glued on to a canvas, or 'assemblages' of made or 'found' items.

Unlike some of his contemporaries, Picasso never went on to create a purely abstract art. In fact his many-sidedness kept him one jump ahead of his admirers, many of whom were taken aback when he returned to more conventional figure painting and then, in the early 1920s, developed a monumental Neo-Classical style. Coincidentally or otherwise, in 1918 he had married the ballerina Olga Koklova and had adopted a prosperous and rather grandly respectable lifestyle – but one which he found increasingly irksome.

In 1925 Picasso began to paint distorted, violently expressive forms that were at least partly a response to personal difficulties. From this time his work became ever more protean, employing – and inventing – a range of styles such as no other artist has attempted. He was also an inventive sculptor (some authorities consider him the 20th century's greatest exponent of the art), and would later take up ceramics with great enthusiasm. In every medium he was enormously prolific, creating over his lifetime tens of thousands of works.

In the late 1930s, when Picasso's creative impulse seemed at last to be flagging, events drove him to create the most celebrated of all his paintings. *Guernica* (page 60) was a direct response to the horrors of the Spanish Civil War. The conflict began in July 1936 with a military coup led by General Francisco Franco, representing the country's fascist, traditionalist and clerical elements, against the Spanish Republic and its elected Popular Front (centre-left) government.

At the outbreak of war, Picasso immediately declared his support for the Republic, raised large sums of money for the cause, and accepted a commission to paint a huge mural for the Spanish pavilion at the 1937 International Exhibition in Paris. Before he had even begun, news arrived that on 26 April 1937 Nazi planes, sent by Hitler to help Franco, had bombed and laid waste the Basque town of Guernica. Picasso set to work at once on preliminary sketches for *Guernica,* and then painted the huge canvas in about a month (May/June 1937). It became the ultimate expression not only of Spanish suffering but of the shattering impact of modern warfare on its victims everywhere.

In spite of everything, the Republicans lost the civil war, and Picasso remained in exile from his native land for the rest of his long life. During World War II he stayed in German-occupied Paris, forbidden to exhibit but not seriously molested.

After the liberation of Paris, Picasso joined the Communist Party, and for a few years some of his works were openly political; but he was also an international celebrity, established in the playground of the rich in the South of France. After a long series of liaisons he finally married for a second time (Jacqueline Roque, 1961) and led an increasingly reclusive life. Artistically prolific to the end, he died on 8 April 1973, at the age of 91.

▷ **The Artist's Father** 1896

Watercolour on paper

REMARKABLY, many great artists and writers have had fathers like Picasso's – pleasant, well-meaning but weak men who never quite manage to maintain their families in a state of middle-class comfort and respectability. José Ruiz Blasco was a dilettante by temperament who was forced in early middle age to eke out a living as a drawing teacher and painter. A few years later, at 42, he compounded his difficulties by marrying and becoming the father of Pablo and two little girls. The young Picasso was deeply ashamed of the family's dependence on richer relatives, and perhaps also of his father's mediocrity as a painter of pigeons. However, thanks to Don José's choice of profession, Picasso never had to face any opposition to his resolve to become an artist, and always had access to a studio and materials.

▷ **The Artist's Mother** 1896

Pastel on paper

PICASSO'S MOTHER, Maria Picasso López, was a strong, vital character who held her family together through many hard times. She was a small, dark, sturdy woman, and Picasso inherited both her frame and her energy, though he sometimes regretted that he had failed to inherit the looks of his tall, fair father. Various interpretations have been put on the fact that he chose to call himself by his mother's name, Picasso, rather than that of his father, José Ruiz Blasco. Picasso himself claimed that he took his mother's name simply because it was a very unusual and striking one. By 1896, when this pastel was done, 15-year-old Picasso had developed into an accomplished artist, set up in his own studio. A year earlier, the family had settled in Spain's most go-ahead, thriving city, Barcelona, which became the scene of Picasso's earliest triumphs.

▷ **Menu from Els Quatre Gats**
1899-1900

IN HIS LATE TEENS, Picasso
rebelled against the academic
style in art, quitting Madrid's
San Fernando Academy and
returning to Barcelona. He
found the stimulus he needed
in the city, at the Els Quatre
Gats (The Four Cats), a
consciously bohemian and
avant-garde tavern. Its
habitués were interested in all
the latest artistic trends in
Paris and London,
particularly the elegant,
undulating art nouveau style.
Picasso became one of the
stars of the establishment,
which was the setting for his
first exhibition of portraits
and caricatures (February
1901). His design for a menu
is influenced by art nouveau,
and also by the bold,
simplified compositions of
poster artists like Henri de
Toulouse-Lautrec and the
British Beggarstaff Brothers.
Appropriately, in 1900 Picasso
set off for London but only
got as far as Paris, where he
would experience an artistic
atmosphere infinitely headier
than anything Barcelona
could offer.

◁ **Child Holding a Dove** 1901

Oil on canvas

PICASSO MADE a brief first visit to Paris in 1900. But it was in the following year that he fell in love with the city, had his first successful exhibition there, and began to collect a band of devoted Parisian friends and followers. From 1904 Paris would be his home for the next four decades. The bold contours and simplified modelling of *Child Holding a Dove,* painted during this decisively important period, reflect the influence of artists such as Gauguin and Cézanne, whose works were still regarded with suspicion by the academic establishment; the touch of sentiment in the painting is Picasso's own. By this time he had rebelled against the social and artistic conformism represented by his father. Yet Don José's slightly absurd partiality for doves and pigeons often reappears in his son's works, right down to the celebrated propaganda dove for the peace movement (page 68) and the 1957 *Pigeons* series (page 73).

◁ **The Poet Sabartés** 1901

Oil on canvas

THIS IS SOMETIMES called *Le Bock* (The Beer) or simply *Portrait of Sabartés;* but Picasso himself insisted on 'the poet' as part of the title. There was a hint of irony in this as a description of Sabartés, and the painting undoubtedly presents him in an exaggeratedly soulful, glamorous light. According to Sabartés, it was painted not long after his arrival in Paris from Spain (October 1901). He was sitting alone in a tavern, in a state of myopic isolation and boredom, until Picasso and some companions suddenly burst into the room and cheered him up. A few days later, in Picasso's studio, Sabartés was shown this painting, which he recognized as portraying 'the spectre of my solitude'. It is arguably the first work of Picasso's 'Blue Period', characterized not only by all-pervasive blue tones but by a preoccupation with suffering, rejection and poverty.

Detail

◁ **Old Jew with a Boy** 1903

Oil on canvas

PAINTED AT THE HEIGHT of Picasso's Blue Period, when his pictures had become steeped in this cold, melancholy-inducing colour. The wretched of the earth – prostitutes, beggars and convicts – people the canvases of the Blue Period, often posed with a premeditated awkwardness that emphasizes their lack of any settled, respectable place in the world. The old Jew, blind, destitute and a member of an outcast race, epitomizes the suffering with which Picasso was obsessed at this time; in true romantic fashion he seems to have believed that, as an artist, he too was doomed to be rejected and despised. The theme of blindness also appears in other pictures, perhaps reflecting Picasso's awareness of his father's deteriorating sight; one interpretation of the figures in this scene is that they represent Don José (page 8) and the young Picasso.

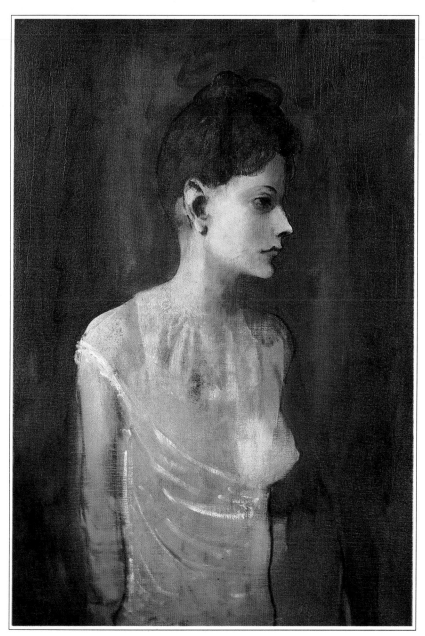

◁ **Woman in a Chemise** 1905

Oil on canvas

IN VIEW OF PICASSO'S mercurial character, both as a man and as an artist, it seems remarkable that his sorrowful Blue Period should have lasted for such a long time, from late 1901 until 1905. Painted with masterful simplicity, *Woman in a Chemise* is a transitional work in a very obvious sense, combining Picasso's habitual blue tones with the pinks that would soon become the hallmark of his new 'Rose' period. As so often in his art, a new style was heralded by the appearance of a new woman in his life. All we know about this one is that her name was Madeleine, and that she became Picasso's mistress and had an abortion in the course of their brief liaison. Replaced in Picasso's affections by Fernande Olivier, who would remain his companion until 1912, Madeleine disappeared and is heard of no more.

▷ Young Acrobat on a Ball
1905

Oil on canvas

BY 1905, Picasso's hardest times were over: after a period of dire poverty, he was beginning to sell his works, he was happy in his relationship with the voluptuous Fernande Olivier, and he lived at the centre of a bohemian band of artists and writers which included Max Jacob, Guillaume Apollinaire and Alfred Jarry. Pinks and ochres predominated in his palette, and the harsh pathos of the Blue Period was replaced by a gentler, though still rather melancholy, mood. Picasso's preferred subjects were now the clowns and acrobats whom he went to see several times a week at the Médrano Circus in Paris; but his paintings of them focus on their rootless existence and incongruous domesticity rather than their professional skills. Here, at least, an acrobatic feat is being performed, but the setting is mysteriously pastoral and the brooding, massive presence of the man gives the picture a curiously intense, uneasy quality.

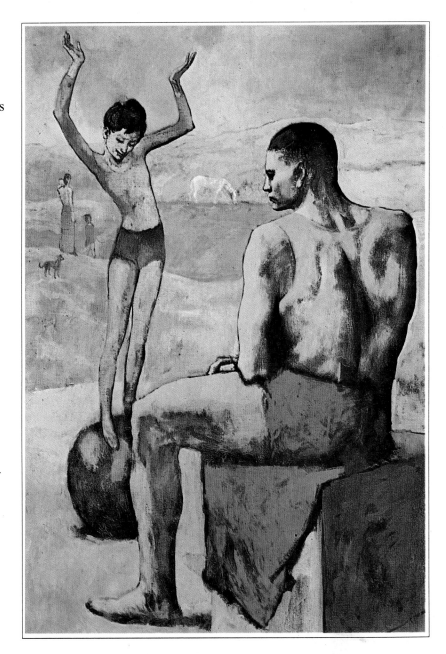

Portrait of Madame Canals 1905

Oil on canvas

◁ *Previous page 17*

DURING HIS EARLY YEARS in Paris, Picasso gradually mastered the French language and made many French friends; one of the earliest was the poet Max Jacob, with whom he shared a room, and some very hard times, as early as the winter of 1902-03. But he also remained close to his fellow-Spaniards in the French capital, among them the Catalan artist Ricardo Canals, now mainly remembered as the man who taught Picasso etching – a not insignificant distinction in view of Picasso's later pre-eminence in this art. Canals's wife was a beautiful Italian, but Picasso portrays her here in traditional Spanish fashion, as an aloof but enticing figure in a mantilla; the treatment of the material is masterly, ranging from meticulous detail to very cursory, Gainsborough-like passages towards the bottom. Picasso's inability to rest on his laurels appears in the contrast between this lovely but conventional work and the 'crude' self-portrait painted the following year (page 20).

▷ **Boy with a Pipe** 1905

Oil on canvas

THIS IS A LOVELY but enigmatic work, painted at some point after Picasso's return from a trip to Holland, in the summer of 1905. The boy is shown against a floral background which may be a screen or a theatre curtain. We do not know why he wears a garland on his head, or why his hand is holding a pipe in an oddly clumsy grip; one suggestion, that it refers to the pleasures of opium, is lent credibility by Fernande Olivier's account of how smoking the drug heightened and intensified her lovemaking with Picasso. Whatever the exact circumstances, *Boy with a Pipe* maintains the mild, reflective mood characteristic of his Rose Period works. These were making Picasso's reputation in Paris and finding willing buyers – in spite of which he broke abruptly with the past and developed a radical new style of painting that would transform the history of 20th-century art.

△ **Self-portrait** 1906

Oil on canvas

THE IMPORTANCE of colour in Picasso's early work is suggested by the universal use of 'Blue' and 'Rose' as handy labels for entire phases of it. Yet suddenly, in this self-portrait and other works of 1906, the colours are restrained to the point of neutrality, and Picasso's painterly skills, so delicately employed in *Boy with a Pipe* (page 18), have been abandoned in favour of a simplified, monumental style. The artist's face is neither a detailed likeness nor a psychological study; instead, it has the masklike aspect and sense of power found in primitive art. And in fact Picasso was being deeply influenced at this time by ancient Iberian stone sculpture. Then in 1906 he and Fernande took a trip to Gosol in northern Spain, and its stark landscape helped to inspire a new style – one with which Picasso would use to lay the foundations of modern art.

▷ **Les Demoiselles d'Avignon** 1907

Oil on canvas

EVEN AT THE TIME, Picasso knew that this was the most important picture he had painted so far. He spent months on preparatory sketches, made major changes even when the work was in progress, and produced a bigger finished canvas than he had ever attempted before. In painting these five ladies from a *maison close* (brothel), Picasso launched a revolt against the entire naturalistic tradition of Western art. Western visual conventions – accurate perspective and a single viewpoint – are violated, for example in the seated woman on the right, seen simultaneously full-face and from behind. The faces of the central figures reflect Picasso's interest in ancient Iberian art; the rest have mask-heads directly inspired by the African sculptures which Picasso had seen in Paris's Musée de l'Homme. The women are monumental, like primitive sculptures, yet there is also a faceting and an emphasis on geometry that hint at Picasso's Cubist future.

◁ **Three Women** 1908

Oil on canvas

PICASSO SHOWED *Les Demoiselles d'Avignon* (page 20) to many of his closest friends and most discriminating patrons, but the painting was so revolutionary that even these members of the avant-garde were stunned and uncomprehending. Not surprisingly, therefore, it was not publicly exhibited for years. But Picasso was not to be diverted from his chosen path, and *Three Women,* though more conventionally harmonious as a composition, is in most respects as shocking as the *Demoiselles.* Apart from the masklike heads, evidently suggested by African sculptures, the all-pervasive redness and the radical simplifications (for example, the spade-like hand of the figure on the left) still have the power to disconcert. So have the uplifted arms, which belong to a pose that is by tradition sexually inviting, but here, as in *Les Demoiselles d'Avignon,* takes on a curiously perfunctory, ritual quality.

Detail

Detail

▷ **Lady with a Fan** 1909

Oil on canvas

IN *Lady with a Fan* Picasso is visibly moving away from the preoccupation with African sculpture and primitivism which had dominated *Les Demoiselles d'Avignon* (page 20) and *Three Women* (page 23). The picture is still notable for its monumental, three-dimensional quality, but its entire feeling is different, and the 'African' figures have been replaced by a female who is discernably dressed in elegant early 20th-century fashion. The geometric elements in the composition derive in part from Paul Cézanne, perhaps the greatest of all the 19th-century forerunners of modern art. Cézanne's death in 1906 had led to a flurry of retrospective exhibitions, and Picasso made a study of the older master's work as part of his own quest for a new direction. He may well have found inspiration not only in Cézanne's paintings but also in his now-celebrated dictum that it was necessary 'to render nature after the cylinder, the sphere and the cone', which might almost be the formula for Cubism.

▷ **Factory at Horta de Ebro** 1909

Oil on canvas

IN 1909 PICASSO took Fernande Olivier on a momentous summer holiday at Horta de Ebro. He knew this mountain village well, since he had stayed there 10 years before with the family of his great friend Manuel Pallarès; it was Picasso's first experience of the countryside, and he later declared grandiloquently, 'Everything I know, I learned in Pallarès's village.' This second visit was a less happy one: the Pallarès family and other villagers were hostile because Picasso and Fernande were not married, and Fernande herself was ill for much of the time. Nevertheless the bleak landscape and bare stuccoed village houses inspired Picasso to push his experimentation a stage further, forging a new style in which visual realities were reduced to their geometrical elements. On his return to Paris, Picasso discovered that his friend Georges Braque had been working along almost identical lines. The two artists formed one of the most celebrated partnerships in the history of art, and Cubism was born.

◁ **Portrait of Ambroise Vollard** 1909-10

Oil on canvas

AMBROISE VOLLARD was one of the most perceptive art dealers of his time, taking up the 19-year-old Pablo Picasso in 1901, almost immediately after his arrival in Paris. The portrait is typical of Cubism in its first phase. It is thinly painted in monochrome pigments, as if Picasso feared that the richness and brilliance of colour might somehow corrupt the purity of his Cubist vision. Because these Cubist works seem cerebral and austere – a largely illusory impression – it is easy to overlook their sheer inventiveness. Though he has apparently been thoroughly deconstructed, Vollard is still perfectly recognizable; but within a year or so Picasso would be painting 'portraits' in which reality was completely submerged and only the occasional visual clue indicated the identity of the sitter. Vollard ceased to be Picasso's dealer from about 1906 to 1927, when the artist began a magnificent set of a hundred etchings, the *Vollard Suite,* which took almost 10 years to complete.

▷ **The Violin** 1912

Oil on canvas

By 1912 controversy over the validity of Cubism was more intense than ever. A number of new recruits had joined Picasso and Braque, notably the young Spanish painter Juan Gris, and the poet Guillaume Apollinaire and other writers were emerging as propagandists for what was now a full-scale artistic movement. Cubist works were grouped and shown in strength at the Salon des Indépendants and other established venues. But the wider public remained unconvinced and, as has so often happened, there were those who found anything new immoral rather than merely unaesthetic: in France's parliament, the Chamber of Deputies, Cubism was denounced as 'anti-artistic and anti-national'. Nowadays, while it is still possible to appreciate how bewildering *The Violin* must have been to a spectator raised on conventional narrative and portrait painting, its lack of patriotism is apparent only in the fact that it was painted by a Spaniard!

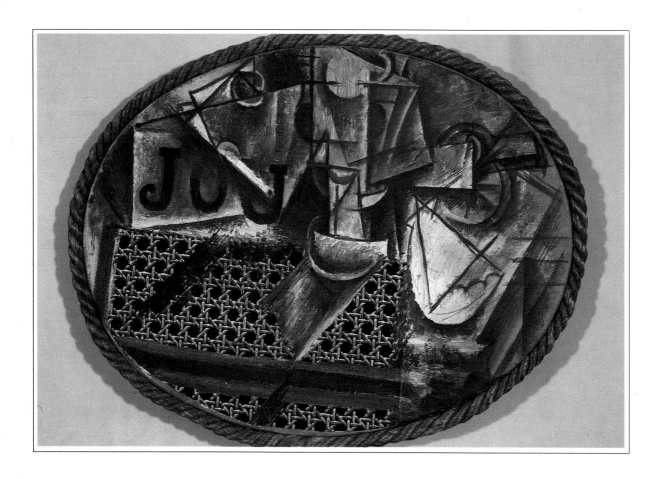

◁ **Still Life with Chair Caning**
1912

Collage

Detail

DURING THEIR collaboration in
the Cubist movement, both
Picasso and Braque reached a
point at which visible realities
were so completely dismantled
and geometrically arranged in
their paintings that they
became virtually invisible.
But in 1912, instead of taking
the final step into abstract art,
the two men preferred to
re-introduce elements from
the real world. However, these
were no longer just painted
images. Braque, for example,
inserted words into his
canvases. In *Still Life with Chair
Caning* Picasso went even
further. The 'frame' is simply a
piece of rope. Most of the
canvas is occupied by a typical
Cubist cafe ensemble (glass,
lemon, newspaper) but the
caning of the chair back is
more conventionally shown –
because it is actually printed
on to a piece of oil cloth that
Picasso stuck on to the canvas,
thereby inventing the collage.
Finally he painted shadows
across the oil cloth, wittily
compounding the confusion
between the 'real' and the
'unreal'.

Detail

▷ **Violin and Grapes** 1912

Oil on canvas

THE STYLE ORIGINALLY pioneered by Picasso and Braque is often described as 'Analytic Cubism', because it involved 'analysing' (or at least breaking up) objects into their geometric components. It was superseded between 1912 and 1915 by 'Synthetic Cubism', in which the artists (joined by Picasso's fellow-Spaniard, Juan Gris) are said to have reversed the process, building up a recognizable image from abstract elements. Putting these technical distinctions aside, it became clear in a work such as *Violin and Grapes* that more varied and lively colour was creeping back into Picasso's work. So were images of the real world, though reassembled with a playful inventiveness which became one of the artist's enduring characteristics. Coincidentally or otherwise, the changes coincided with new developments in Picasso's personal life: Fernande had left him in 1911, and shortly afterwards he fell in love with Marcelle Humbert, whom he called 'Eva'. Picasso's fondness for the guitar as an artistic subject probably owes less to his Spanishness than to its sensuous plasticity, and in particular to its distinctly feminine contours.

▷ **Portrait of Olga in an Armchair** 1917

Oil on canvas

THE OUTBREAK of World War I in August 1914 ended Picasso's partnership with Georges Braque, who was called up to serve in the army. Although Picasso, as a Spanish citizen, did not have to become a combatant, he was affected by the changed atmosphere in Paris, and then devastated by the death of his companion, Eva, who succumbed to tuberculosis. His spirits revived when the writer Jean Cocteau recruited him to design the decor and costumes of *Parade,* a daring modernist production by Serge Diaghilev's celebrated Russian Ballet. Working on the project in Rome, Picasso found himself exhilarated by the city and its classic tradition, and by the physical beauty of the dancers. He fell in love with one of them, Olga Koklova, who became his wife in July 1918. This exquisite portrait, combining meticulous detail with a cursorily finished background, gives the measure of Picasso's mastery of conventional techniques, which were about to assume a new importance in his work.

▷ **The Bathers** 1918

Oil on canvas

DESPITE ITS PLAYFUL distortions of the human form, this scene has all the wind-blown freshness of a seaside poster. It is worth recalling that swimming in the sea was uncommon, and sunbathing unheard of, until after World War I. The physical freedom and unselfconscious display of these girls was also new, and although they have not yet bobbed their hair they can be regarded as early examples of the liberated 'flapper'. So, uncharacteristically, Picasso's canvas records a change in social fashions, although this was not necessarily his intention in painting it. He himself became a devotee of the beach. *The Bathers* was inspired by a visit to Biarritz, after which he spent his summers by the sea, later pioneering the popularity of now-famous resorts such as Juan les Pins and St Tropez. Sun-drenched photographs of Picasso's stocky, bare-chested figure, accompanied by the muse of the moment, made him the only 20th-century artist whom millions of people could instantly recognize.

▷ **Still Life on a Chest of Drawers** 1919

Oil on canvas

STILL LIFE, an arrangement of objects completely under the artist's control, was the main vehicle for Picasso's Cubism, although unlike his friend and partner Braque he did also sometimes apply the Cubist fragmentation of reality to portraiture. From 1917 he returned to a more realistic style in paintings such as *Portrait of Olga in an Armchair* (page 34), while simultaneously continuing to produce Cubist works. Here, unusually, he has tackled a still life in a relatively traditional, non-Cubist vein. But Picasso almost never lets us forget that what we are looking at is man-made, deliberately undermining any 'photographic' aspect of his works by leaving unfinished patches and cross-hatchings. The elegantly severe wall-mouldings may hint at the artist's growing interest in classicism; or perhaps they only reflect the comfortable and respectable life-style that Picasso had adopted after his marriage to Olga.

◁ **The Village Dance** 1921-2

Oil on canvas

By 1921 PICASSO'S years of financial struggle were over, and he was now famous. Ironically, the reputation of this Spanish artist was boosted by two big sales of works which the French government had confiscated during the war from Picasso's former dealers, Kahnweiler and Uhde, who had the misfortune to be German-born. While producing both Cubist and more traditional work, he was also developing a new 'Neo-Classical' style, featuring figures reminiscent of antique statues but of extraordinary bulk and largeness of limb. Here, however, the size of the figures seems designed to emphasize their rusticity, and their modern clothes sit awkwardly on them. Such clothing is rarely represented in Picasso's paintings, highlighting the curious fact that this artist – still the epitome of everything 'modern' and distinctively 20th century – preferred to perform his transformations on hallowed images from the past such as the nude, the harlequin or acrobat, and the still life of fruits and flowers.

▷ Harlequin 1923

Oil on canvas

DURING HIS LONG CAREER Picasso returned time and again to the traditional figure of Harlequin. In his alternative roles as a resourceful scoundrel (in the Commedia dell'Arte theatre) or acrobat (in the circus) Harlequin's gaily costumed figure is not only picturesque, but also embodies the contradiction of which artists are all too keenly aware, between the creator of illusions of beauty and mirth and the vulnerable human being behind the greasepaint. In his youth Picasso showed Harlequin as a circus performer; later, the diamond-patterned Harlequin costume added to the gaiety of the two celebrated versions of the Cubist *Three Musicians* (1921). Then in February 1923 Picasso persuaded the Catalan painter Jacinto Salvado to pose for the first of a series of Harlequin paintings. His solemn expression and rather stiff pose are out of keeping with the vivid, outlandish hat and costume; the incongruity would be even more marked if the painting were not in an intriguingly 'unfinished' state.

▷ **Seated Woman** 1923

Oil on canvas

THIS IS ONE OF the masterworks of Picasso's Neo-Classical phase, which lasted for only a brief period in the early 1920s. As in the *Portrait of Olga in an Armchair* (page 34), these Neo-Classical images were recognizable – there was no hint of Cubism – but they no longer meticulously recorded appearances, and they belonged to no definable place or time. The figures Picasso painted in this style had the stature and proportions of giants, with slab-like torsos and under-articulated limbs, hands and feet. Their apparent clumsiness and simplified features sometimes verged on caricature (as in *The Village Dance,* page 38), but other examples achieve the monumental quality and sense of calm grandeur that have long represented the ideal of classicism. *Seated Woman*, in her simple shift, is one of these, at once timeless and unmistakably a product of modernity.

The Pipes of Pan 1923

Oil on canvas

◁ Previous page 41

THE PIPES OF PAN belongs to an element in the classical tradition that has always had a surprising appeal for European poets and artists. This is the pastoral, Mediterranean world of simple, sunlit pleasures and amorous shepherds and shepherdesses; its music, equally simple and uncomplicated, is that of the pan pipes. Civilized people turn to pastoral when they are tired of sophistication and complexity; in other words, pastoral is a form of classical primitivism, gentler in mood than the primitivism that looks to non-European cultures. Picasso has expressed all this in modern terms in a canvas of great poetic simplicity. The human figures are no longer shepherds but young men in bathing trunks. A horizon distinguishes between sea and sky as schematically as the rectangular blocks which form the rest of the background, much in the style of a theatre set. If the boy on the right has been playing, he has now stopped, and the scene is filled with a great calm and a great silence.

▷ The Lovers 1923

Oil on canvas

PURITY OF LINE and colour, economy of means, ideal figures and an atmosphere of nobility and restrained emotion – these are the admired characteristics of classicism in all ages, based on the qualities ascribed to ancient Greek and Roman art. In *The Lovers,* Picasso probably comes as close to classical perfection as it is possible for a modern artist to do without any direct imitation of the past. There is a theatrical element in the painting (the lovers may well have been 'frozen' to form a tableau as the curtain comes down at the end of an act), reminiscent of the classical tradition derived from the French dramatist Racine rather than from the ancients. Picasso had in fact been immersed in theatrical activity ever since his involvement with Diaghilev and *Parade* (page 34), and many paintings of this period, including the celebrated *Pipes of Pan* could easily be interpreted as stage scenes.

◁ **Paul as a Harlequin** 1924

Oil on canvas

PAUL, PICASSO'S FIRST CHILD, was born in February 1921. As with his other family portraits, notably that of his wife Olga (page 34), Picasso adopts a meticulous representational technique which leaves us in no doubt that this is exactly what the child looked like. But he undermines the illusionism of the painting by leaving large areas of the canvas sketchy or unpainted; even Paul's feet, and the ruff round his neck, are only drawn in. This is a deliberately subversive technique. However naturalistic his style on certain occasions, Picasso always held to a central belief of the modern artist: that the work of art is not a copy of reality but an addition to it, an independent entity subject to its own inner laws. *Paul as a Harlequin* is one of a series of canvases in which Picasso portrayed the little boy, often in fancy dress as a pierrot or a bullfighter.

◁ **Three Dancers** 1925

Oil on canvas

THIS IS A VERY LARGE picture – which, in Picasso's case, means that it almost certainly announces a change of direction. The style and subject matter provide ample confirmation. After years of classical restraint, it is as if Picasso can stand no more and has allowed his suppressed rage and anguish to erupt on to the canvas. Like *The Lovers* (page 42), *Three Dancers* is theatrical; but now the bodies are violently distorted (an emotional distortion, quite different from the 'analytical' distortions of Picasso's Cubist works) and the harsh colours and angularities suggest that some grotesque ritual is being enacted. The central dancer, it has been said, looks like a crucified figure. There were certainly personal factors behind this change of style (bitter conflicts had developed between Picasso and Olga). The violence and expressive distortions – especially of the female figure – continued into the late 1920s, leading many critics to interpret this as a period of misogyny.

▷ **The Studio** 1928

Oil on canvas

NOTHING COULD BETTER illustrate Picasso's inexhaustibly varied genius than this picture, so 'out of character' in its apparent lack of any subject. Its general organization suggests that Picasso intended a private matching of strengths with the Dutch artist Piet Mondrian, whose abstract style was similarly based on flat, bright colours and compartmentalized geometric shapes. But in Picasso's painting there is a subject – the artist in his studio – although most of its components have been brilliantly rendered with a few lines, reminiscent of the wire sculpture that was beginning to interest Picasso at about the same time. On the left stands the artist, his easel indicated only by a circle (standing for the thumb-hole) and his poised brush by a single diagonal line. His models are a jug or bowl and a white marble or plaster bust which stand on a table covered with a red cloth. This virtuoso canvas is executed in a style to which Picasso never returned, and is consequently unique among his works.

▷ **The Sculptor** 1931

Oil on plywood

FROM THE 1920s Picasso felt
free to distort and disassemble
the forms of human beings
and objects, at will rather than
as part of an artistic
programme such as Cubism.
More than ever,
metamorphosis became the
most obvious characteristic of
his work; often, especially in
the late 1920s, it served to
express violent feelings by
peopling the canvas with
monsters – especially women.
By contrast, *The Sculptor* seems
to have been conceived in a
playful spirit, though its
subject was one to which
Picasso would return again
and again: the artist at work or
contemplating his work, alone
or in the company of his
model, who is also his lover.
Here there is no model – only
two sculptures, apparently in
very different styles – but the
erotic feeling expressed by
their curving contours is
unmistakable. The sculptor's
countenance integrates profile
and full face in a skilful, witty
fashion that became one of
Picasso's hallmarks.

▷ **Girl before a Mirror** 1932

Oil on canvas

THE GIRL IS PICASSO' latest love, Marie Thérèse Walther, a statuesque blonde whom the painter met in 1927, when he was 46 and she only 17. For several years the affair remained a secret: so much so that Marie Thérèse hardly figured in Picasso's work, normally so charged with autobiographical fact and fantasy. But by 1932 the secret was out, and this painting is one of several in which the artist celebrated her youth and loveliness. Picasso most often shows her as sunk in her own rounded, opulent flesh, either dreamily compliant or actually asleep. Here, however, Marie Thérèse takes a more active role, contemplating her image in a long mirror. In legend and folk tale the mirror often shows more than a faithful reversed image of the gazer, and the difference between the two images of the girl in this picture is striking; it suggests among other things that the mirror image is Marie Thérèse's dark side or Freudian unconscious.

▷ **The Minotaur** 1933

Collage

Detail

THIS IS A REMARKABLE example of Picasso's ability to combine a wide range of materials, including ordinary objects such as corrugated paper, doilies and foil, into a single, well-integrated composition. Moreover he has also incorporated into it his own drawing of a Minotaur, a mythical beast that had come to have a special significance for him. In Greek legend the Minotaur was a monstrous creature, with the head of a bull and the body of a man, who lived deep in a labyrinth in Knossos, the chief city of ancient Crete; Greek youths and maidens were regularly given to him as sacrifices until he was slain by the hero Theseus. In his many appearances in Picasso's art the Minotaur is a terrifying figure, capable of murder and rape, yet not so much good or evil as a kind of force of nature; significantly, Picasso himself identified with the beast. In photographic form the collage was used as the front page of a magazine, *Minotaure*.

MINOTAURE

▷ The Bullfight: Death of the Torero 1933

Oil on panel

LIKE MANY SPANIARDS, Picasso saw his first bullfights when he was still a child perched on his father's knee. His earliest surviving painting (done when he was eight) is of a picador, the horseman who drives a lance into the bull in order to weaken it before the final phase of the spectacle. The passion was a lifelong one, despite Picasso's long absences from his native land, but two visits to Spain in the early 1930s evidently played a part in reintroducing the corrida into his art. In this painting, and in its companion of the same year, *Death of the Female Toreador,* Picasso portrayed not the death of the bull – the normal culmination of the ritual – but one of those rarer occasions when the matador was fatally gored. By contrast, the death of the picador's horse, its entrails dangling, was a commonplace event; but Picasso fused the two into a single scene, all the more intense for almost overfilling the picture area.

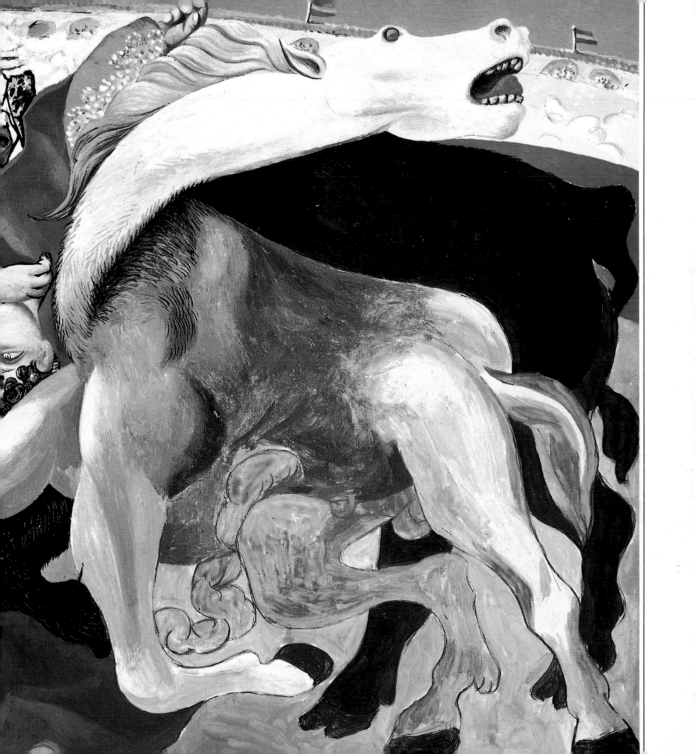

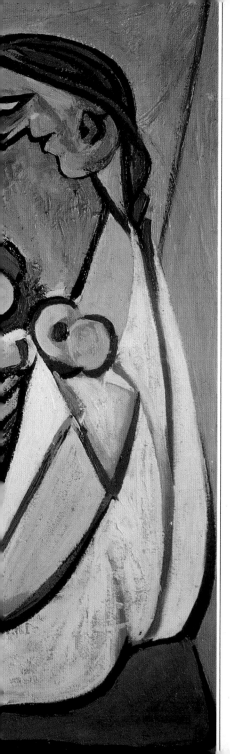

◁ **The Muse** 1935

Oil on canvas

ALSO KNOWN, perhaps more appropriately, as *Young Woman Drawing*, and also as *Two Women*. One woman sits, apparently copying what she sees in the mirror set up in front of her, while the other sleeps with her head in her arms. The Muse is the best-known of a series of paintings executed by Picasso at this time, showing young women drawing, writing or reading. The rounded, ample forms associated with his passion for Marie Thérèse Walther have been replaced by an angular style which is here almost vertiginous in its effect. The sleeping girl still resembles Marie Thérèse, and indeed she would have a share in Picasso's affections for some years to come (their daughter Maia was born a few months after this was painted, in October 1935). But the 'other woman', already present in this painting, would soon also appear in Picasso's life.

◁ **Woman in a Hat** 1935

Oil on canvas

PICASSO HAS GIVEN this woman a curious, bird-like face which is difficult to take entirely seriously, and there is more than a suspicion of a dig at haute couture in the masterly reduction of the sitter's person and dress to a few simple components. The good humour of the painting is all the more remarkable in that Picasso was going through what he later called 'the worst period of my life'. His wife Olga had finally left him, messy divorce proceedings seemed imminent, and his emotional life was in confusion. The extremity of his distress was shown by the fact that, at 53, the ever-prolific Picasso found himself unable to paint, a condition that lasted for about nine months (May 1935 to February 1936). But his compulsive creativity was not to be denied, and during this difficult time Picasso began to write poetry that has since become widely admired for its inventive Surrealist vein.

◁ **Portrait of Dora Maar** 1937

EARLY IN 1936 the poet Paul Eluard introduced Picasso to a 30-year-old photographer and painter named Dora Maar, who rapidly became the most important woman in his life. A strong and serious character, Dora was, unlike Olga and Marie Thérèse Walther, able to understand and even help with Picasso's work. However, Picasso's relationship with Marie Thérèse continued, and for years he alternated visits to Marie Thérèse and her daughter Maia with trips to the South of France and elsewhere in which he was accompanied by Dora Maar. His many portraits of Dora are recognizably related to one another: her dark good looks, round chin and long painted fingernails, themselves highly distinctive, are heightened by Picasso's angular treatment and use of dramatic blacks and reds. As always, Picasso's life and work were so closely intertwined that the equation 'new woman = new style' became virtually axiomatic.

Guernica 1937

Oil on canvas

◁ *Previous pages 58-59*

THIS HUGE WORK was conceived and painted as Picasso's response to the destruction of the small Basque town of Guernica by Nazi aircraft; the political context and circumstances are more fully described in the Introduction. Dora Maar found Picasso a studio in Paris big enough to hold the projected work, and photographed each stage of its creation. *Guernica's* impact is intensified by its great size and the fact that it is painted entirely in black, white and shades of grey. Picasso's techniques and many of his images are to be found in earlier works, but here they are integrated into a great cry of shock and pain. The bombs are invisible, their impact hinted at in the sunflash of the electric bulb and a flare of light above a door; we see only the victims, suddenly struck down. *Guernica* was the highlight of the Paris Exhibition, after which it toured internationally, helping to create sympathy for the beleaguered Spanish Republic; but, like most works of art, it finally failed to change the course of events.

▷ **Weeping Woman** 1937

Oil on canvas

PICASSO'S INTENSIVE work on *Guernica* gave rise to emotional and artistic reverberations which lasted well into the autumn of 1937. He became obsessed with images of weeping women – no longer the blasted and shocked figures of his great painting, but creatures devastated by grief for lost loved ones or unhinged by some tragedy they had witnessed or heard about. Dora Maar was the model for this *Weeping Woman,* her fancy headgear perhaps indicating that she is a chic Parisienne, normally indifferent to such matters, who has just been brought face to face with the terrible realities of her time. The woman's strange eyes, the jagged lines like broken glass and the pallor of the lower part of her face, the teardrops doubling as fingernails, the bared teeth and the bitten handkerchief all work to make this one of Picasso's most harrowing images.

▷ **Night Fishing at Antibes**
1939

Oil on canvas

THE SUBJECT of this painting was based on Picasso's observation of night scenes off the shore at Antibes in the South of France, where men went out and fished by the light of acetylene lamps; the lights attracted the fish to the surface, where they could be netted or speared. The human population of this colourful, singularly whimsical work is oddly grotesque: the fishermen look half-witted, while the girls strolling on the quay (one wheeling a bicycle and licking a double ice-cream cone) seem utterly vacuous. The painting has not pleased all the critics, perhaps because it is not as portentous as its large size suggests it ought to be. Picasso finished it just as World War II was breaking out but, although some ingenious interpretations of it have been put forward, it seems to contain little of the prophetic 'relevance' that is often naïvely expected of an artist at such a moment.

Detail

▷ **Portrait of Sabartés** 1939

Oil on canvas

THIS IS JAIME SABARTÉS, the glamorous, dreamy 'poet' of the 1901 portrait (page 13), now a man in late middle age. Picasso's friend ever since their early days together in Barcelona and Paris, Sabartés had responded to an appeal from the artist in 1935, when the separation from Olga and other complications had brought Picasso close to despair. Having left Spain to help Picasso through his difficulties, Sabartés stayed on as his secretary and companion for the rest of his life. Picasso painted and drew his friend in many guises. Here he is a ruffed 16th-century Spanish gentleman – perhaps a sly dig at his function as chief courtier to King Pablo, for Picasso certainly had a capricious and cruel side to his nature. The painting was done at Royan, a town on the Atlantic coast where Picasso and his entourage established themselves a few days after the outbreak of war.

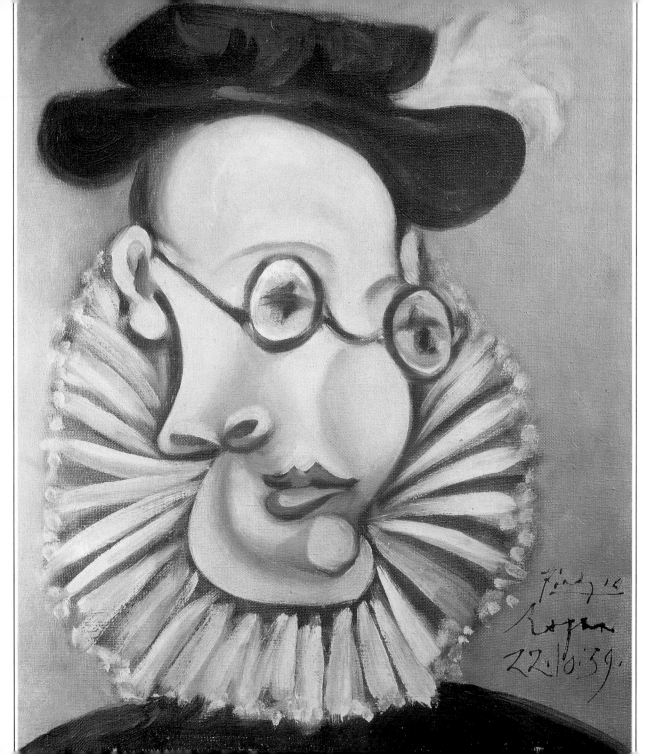

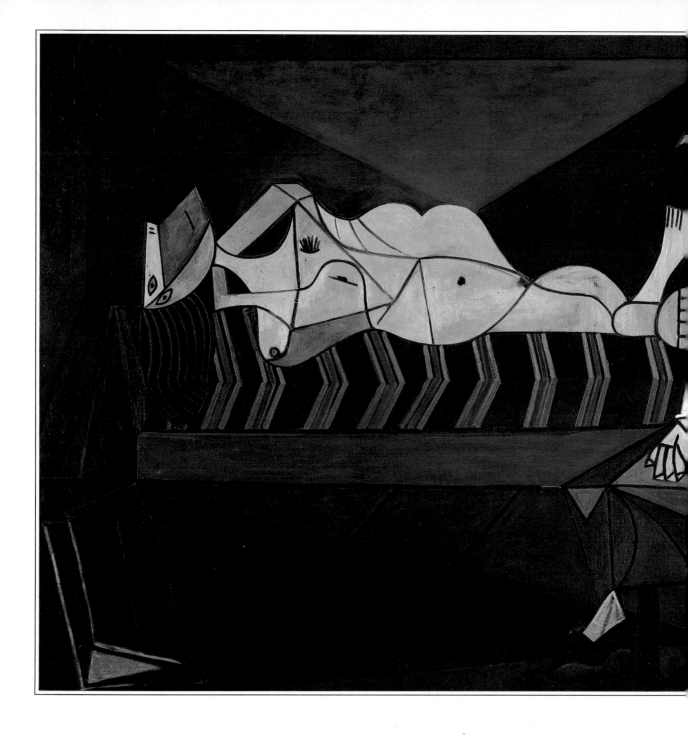

◁ **Aubade** 1942

Oil on canvas

PICASSO STAYED on in the little town of Royon until the Germans invaded and overran France in the summer of 1940. Then, despite offers of refuge abroad, he chose to return to Paris, living in the capital all through the Occupation. He remained aloof from the conquerors; when a German officer spotted a photograph of *Guernica* (page 60) in his studio and asked 'Did you do that?' Picasso is said to have replied 'No, you did!' During the war his art was not overtly political, but the oppressiveness of its atmosphere can still be sensed. *Aubade* combines rather strangely the traditionally pleasant theme, of a lady being serenaded, with a distinct feeling of darkness and claustrophobia; and neither the mandolin player, all cutting edges, nor the nude, all too reminiscent of meat on a slab, are happy figures. After the Liberation, Picasso returned to the vein of *Guernica* to record the impact of the Nazi death camps in *The Charnel House* (1944-5).

△ **Dove for the Festival of Youth** 1949

Lithograph

IN OCTOBER 1944 Picasso joined the Communist Party, which had an outstanding record in the wartime French Resistance and would remain a force in French politics for several decades. Once more, a new departure in Picasso's life coincided with the arrival of a new woman, in this instance the painter Françoise Gilot, herself a committed Communist. Over the next few years Picasso supported the peace movement (in Western eyes little more than a Communist 'front') by attending congresses and also by providing the movement with this, its celebrated dove symbol. In the 1950s he painted a number of ambitious political canvases such as *Massacre in Korea*. Ironically, Picasso's works were regularly denounced as decadent by the Soviet media, since they failed to conform to the approved 'Socialist Realist' style promoted throughout the Communist world. After the mid-1950s politics virtually disappeared from Picasso's art, although he remained a party member until his death in 1973.

▷ **Portrait of a Painter, after El Greco** 1950

Oil on canvas

PICASSO FELT A LIFELONG admiration for Spanish masters such as El Greco and Velázquez, and ultimately a sense of rivalry with them too. Both were intensely and distinctively Spanish – El Greco in spite of the fact that he was born in Crete (hence El Greco, 'the Greek') and arguably brought with him to his adopted country some elements of the ancient Byzantine tradition. El Greco's impact on Picasso began early, and one of the 16th-century painter's mannerisms, his elongated figures, certainly influenced the Blue Period figures and some later works. *Portrait of a Painter* is a playful reworking of one of El Greco's portraits, suggesting the ruff and dark Spanish costume but making free with every other element in the original. This is an early example of a pursuit that would become an obsession with Picasso – 'copying', or rather turning into Picassos, the great paintings of the past.

▷ **Skull of a Goat, Bottle and Candle** 1952

Oil on canvas

DURING THIS PERIOD, heads and skulls of goats seem to have fascinated Picasso; they appear not only in paintings and drawings, but also in his sculptures. Here he has actually used one of his own works, an assemblage, as the model for a still-life painting. Instead of single lines, wide bands serve as contours, giving a distinctive effect rather like stained glass. In combination with the black-grey-white colour scheme, they create a notably sinister impression, focusing attention on the most highly articulated object in the picture – the skull, which is of course a traditional symbol of mortality, just as the candle, burning down while its flame is endangered by every breath of air, conventionally represents the transience of life. So, in a startling, expressive fashion Picasso has renewed one of the historic functions of the still life, as a reminder that nothing lasts and death is never very far away.

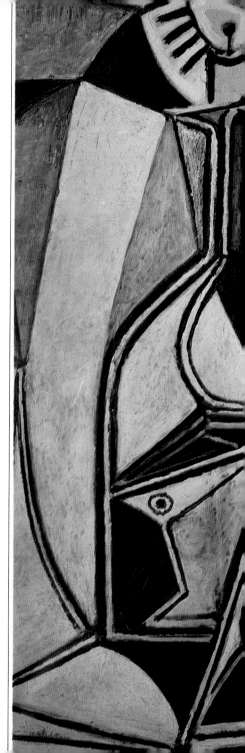

◁ **Portrait of Jacqueline** 1957

Oil on canvas

Picasso's emotional life remained turbulent well into old age. In 1953 Françoise Gilot left him, taking with her Claude and Paloma, her two children by Picasso. Not long afterwards he met Jacqueline Roque, and in 1955 they went to live at La Californie, a villa just outside Cannes. Over the years that followed, Picasso made hundreds of portraits of Jacqueline, whose strong features and dark hair make her easy to identify despite the variety of styles in which Picasso worked; she even modelled characters in famous paintings which he reinterpreted, notably *The Women of Algiers* (Delacroix), *Lola de Valence* (Manet) and *L'Arlésienne* (van Gogh). In 1961 Picasso and Jacqueline married and moved into Notre Dame de Vie at Mougins, which was to be Picasso's final home. He worked there in increasing seclusion, shielded from the pressures of his celebrity by the relative isolation of the house and by Jacqueline, whose role has been variously interpreted as protective and domineering.

▷ **The Pigeons, Cannes** 1957

Oil on canvas

IN 1957 PICASSO painted a series of views from the window of his studio at La Californie, with pigeons clustered about and the sea and sky in the distance. During this phase of his career he seemed to be measuring himself against the art of the past, and the series was done at about the same time as his ambitious *Las Meniñas* cycle (page 75). *The Pigeons, Cannes* belongs to the tradition of painting associated with artists such as Matisse and Bonnard, much of whose work evokes the physical pleasures and sunlit happiness of southern climes. Matisse created a number of pictures with brilliantly colourful views through open windows, seen from a cool, dark interior. After Matisse's death in 1954 Picasso is reported to have said 'I have to paint for both of us now.' But even in *The Pigeons* Picasso's more restless spirit has not been subdued.

◁ **Las Meniñas** 1957

Oil on canvas

THIS IS ONE OF many Picasso paintings of the 1950s which rework classics from the past in a drastically dissimilar modern idiom. *Las Meniñas* ('The Maids'), by the 17th-century Spanish artist Diego Velázquez, shows the Spanish Infanta (eldest daughter of the king), still a child, with her maids of honour, looking at an artist at work in front of his easel. The picture is seen from the point of view of the royal couple whom Velázquez is painting, themselves visible only in a mirror behind him. For all the differences in style between Velázquez and Picasso, all the elements in the original can still be identified in the brilliantly schematized, jewel-like 20th-century picture, perhaps the finest of

Detail

the *Las Meniñas* series – no less than 44 works – which he painted in the space of a few months.

Detail

▷ **Bust of a Woman, after Cranach** 1958

Colour linocut

HERE PICASSO reinterprets a painting by the 16th-century artist Lucas Cranach the Younger; part of its attraction seems to have been the elaborateness of the woman's costume, the rich fabrics and the lavish ornaments. Almost inevitably, the rather stuffy dignity of the subject undergoes a transformation at Picasso's hands. His version is a gaudy and nervous one in which he once more depicts the human face in neatly integrated frontal and profile views; among other things, this enables the spectator to focus on the face in two different ways and perceive two different expressions on it. The quality of this work, apparently 'crude' yet bursting with energy, owes a good deal to the linocut technique which Picasso used to make it – just one more example of his urge to experiment which, even at the age of 69, remained as powerful as ever.

◁ **The Artist at Work** 1965

Oil on canvas

THE AUTOBIOGRAPHICAL element in Picasso's art was always strong, although it served as a mirror for his feelings and fantasies rather than as a direct record of events. Subjects to which he returned again and again, were the artist at work and the artist and his model. Most often, as in the *Vollard Suite* etchings, the model was also his lover, so that the interlocking of life and art became even more complete – Picasso did in fact feel that artistic and sexual potency were closely related. The waning of his sexual powers from the mid-1960s is perhaps reflected in the solitary state of the artist in this painting; if Picasso nevertheless remained compulsively creative, the strong and violent images of passion in his late works seem like painful memories. He cannot be said to have grown old gracefully: his final self-portrait, painted the year before he died in 1973, is a bleak study of a condemned man, apparently unconsoled by a lifetime of high achievement.

ACKNOWLEDGEMENTS

The Publisher would like to thank the following for their kind permission to reproduce the paintings in this book:

Bridgeman Art Library, London/Giraudon/Musée Picasso, Barcelona 8, 65; **/Giraudon/Musée Picasso, Paris** 30, 34, 36-37, 38, 41, 44, 48, 52-53, 57; **/Giraudon/Prado, Madrid** 58-59 **Giraudon/Private Collection** 56; **/Hermitage, St. Petersburg** 22, 26-27, **Index/Museo Picasso, Barcelona** 9, 10, 17; **/John Hay Whitney Collection** 19; **/Musée Picasso, Paris** cover; **/Museo Picasso, Barcelona** 8; **/Museum of Modern Art, New York** 21, 33, 46-47, 49, 51, 62-67; **/Musée National d'Art Moderne, Paris** 54-55; **/National Gallery of Art, Washington D.C.** 43; **/Philadelphia Museum of Art, Pennsylvania, USA** 20; **/Pushkin Museum, Moscow** 12, 14, 16, 25, 29, 39; **/Tate Gallery, London** 15, 40, 45, 61